Original title:
Charmed by the Charm

Copyright © 2025 Creative Arts Management OÜ
All rights reserved.

Author: Rory Fitzgerald
ISBN HARDBACK: 978-1-80586-062-4
ISBN PAPERBACK: 978-1-80586-534-6

The Mysteries Within

In a quiet room where secrets play,
Odd socks dance in a silly display.
The cat wears a hat, feeling quite grand,
As the goldfish conducts a tiny band.

Llamas in pajamas, what a wild sight,
While pumpkin spice lattes take to flight.
A snail in a shell whispers tales so grand,
Of treasures and treasures, all made of sand.

Echoes of Enchantment

A giraffe wearing glasses reads a book,
While hamsters give squirrels the a look.
Under the table, a worm and a mouse,
Are planning to take over the house.

Meanwhile, the toaster dreams of gold,
While toasting adventures, tales untold.
With buttered popcorn floating through air,
The fridge hums a tune without a care.

Captivated by the Horizon

A walrus in wonder plays checkers with ants,
Wearing a monocle, shared secret chants.
In a field of daisies, frogs do ballet,
As ducks with top hats saunter away.

The moon spins tales to the stars up high,
While clouds play bingo in the night sky.
A squirrel with dreams of chocolate galore,
Invites his pals for a dance on the floor.

Resonate with the Stars

Ninja llamas leap from trees to the ground,
While frogs serenade with a jazz-loving sound.
The refrigerator whispers recipes sweet,
As cupcakes do pirouettes, oh what a feat!

A hedgehog in sneakers races the breeze,
While ants on a mission march with great ease.
Fireflies twinkle a disco delight,
As the moon joins the party, shining so bright.

Enchanted Whispers

In a village where silly hats soar,
Laughter breaks out, never a bore.
A frog in a tie begins to recite,
Tales of the moon and a pickle fight.

Under a tree, the squirrels convene,
Debating the best dance moves they've seen.
With acorns for hats, they tap to the beat,
As the rhythm of giggles fills up the street.

Spellbound Serenade

A cat strums her lute with flair,
While dogs gather round, nodding in the air.
The parrot jumps in with colorful lines,
Making the headlines with chatter that shines.

The mice, in tuxedos, are taking a bow,
As the moonlight reflects on some cheese-made vows.
With confetti of dreams floating all around,
They twirl and they spin on this mystical ground.

Allure of the Unseen

A hidden garden of giggles awaits,
Where flowers wear glasses and chat about dates.
The hedgehogs play poker; they bet their best quills,
While the bunnies bake cookies with dancing frills.

There's a mysterious door that nobody sees,
Guarded by gnomes who beg for some cheese.
They trade tales of moonlight with laughs and a spin,
As magic unfolds, let the fun now begin!

Captivated in Dreamlight

A jester in pajamas, what a sight to behold,
With tricks and with giggles that never grow old.
His juggling is clumsy but full of delight,
Bringing joy to the stage from morning to night.

The clouds above rain down jellybean dreams,
While children all cheer, bursting at the seams.
As laughter erupts and the fun reaches high,
They float on their hopes, like balloons in the sky.

The Art of Enchantment

A wink from a cat, oh what a sight,
It makes you giggle, fills you with light.
With hats made of cheese and shoes that squeak,
Reality bends when the strange things speak.

A dance with a broom, it twirls so grand,
While giggling gnomes lend a helping hand.
The moon plays tricks, wears a silly grin,
And laughter erupts where the fun begins.

Glittering Veils of Mystery

A sparkly dragon flies past your nose,
In a tutu that flutters, it's quite the pose.
It offers you cupcakes that sprout rainbow sprinkles,
And winks like a winker—a joke that clinkles.

Beneath the bright stars, shadows hop and prance,
Each twirl and each twist feels like a dance.
The riddles they whisper are silly and sweet,
As the world spins around on whimsical feet.

Whimsical Shadows at Dusk

As shadows grow long, they start to play,
With marshmallow bunnies that bounce on the fray.
They giggle and chortle, with eyes full of cheer,
Each step that you take brings the silliness near.

A waltz with a lamp post, oh what a thrill,
While squirrels crack jokes that make the heart spill.
With every twinkle from stars up above,
The nighttime laughs echo, as if all in love.

The Spell of Simple Pleasures

A spoon plays the fiddle, oh what a sound,
As cookies join in, twirling round and round.
With jellybean jugglers and syrupy slides,
On the backs of the giggles, the entire world rides.

Bubbles of laughter float high in the air,
Pop one and hear the secrets they share.
Each chortle a potion, each smile a treat,
In a world where the silly makes life feel complete.

Allure of the Invisible

In the corner, a ghost whispers,
With mischief and giggles galore.
Invisible hats are floating,
And jokes that are hard to ignore.

A cat in a bowtie prances,
With a dance of peculiar grace.
Everyone stops to admire,
A spectacle no one can trace.

Playful shadows chase each other,
Under the moon's silvery beam.
A ripple of laughter surrounds,
As reality bends like a dream.

So let the unseen enchant you,
In laughter and whimsy we play.
For magic lives in the shadows,
Where the invisible flirts all day.

Intrigue in Every Glance

With a wink that could launch a rocket,
And a chuckle just shy of a grin.
Every glance holds a secret,
A riddle where nonsense can win.

Like a lion with shoes on its paws,
Each moment is bursting with cheer.
You can't help but tiptoe around,
As laughter makes worries disappear.

Glimpses of oddities sparkle,
As if the world's breaking the rules.
With each turn and twist of fate,
We're just silly, whimsical fools.

In this dance of curious eyes,
Mirth wraps around every heart.
An intrigue both joyous and bright,
Where the absurd becomes an art.

Magical Moments Unfold

A hat tricks a rabbit with ease,
While socks start a riotous dance.
Each moment is sprinkled with giggles,
In a play of pure happenstance.

A tea party hosted by ducks,
Where they sip on the finest of brews.
The pastries are all made of giggles,
And riddles are served with the blues.

As balloons start to whisper and sway,
And the moon wears a jester's hat.
These moments are drawn like a sketch,
On a canvas of silly and fat.

With every tick of the clock,
A tickle, a poke, and a grin.
For in whimsical magic we twirl,
Let the joyous fun begin!

The Captivation of Whimsy

Whimsical wind carries laughter,
Through the branches of a tall tree.
Where the squirrels debate on fashion,
And the flowers hum joyfully.

A dance-off of dandelions,
With their seeds drifting soft in the air.
Each flutter is filled with delight,
As the world becomes light as a chair.

Marbles roll with a ticklish sound,
And giggles race past clouds of fluff.
Every step is another rainbow,
Making mundane stuff feel quite tough.

In this curious carnival show,
Where whimsy is never outdone.
We find joy in the odd and the strange,
As laughter and nonsense both run.

The Embers of Possibility

In a world where socks mismatch,
A cat wears a tiny hat,
Dancing under twinkling stars,
All the wishes seem where they're at.

A donut rolled down the street,
It squeaked—a true pastry knight!
Defending crumbs with great delight,
Oh, the mischief's out for a treat!

Silly quirks breed wild delight,
A frog hops in a goldfish bowl,
With a splash, it takes a flight,
To the land that knows no control.

In the glow of the moonlit cheer,
Jellybeans argue with marshmallows,
A kingdom led by sprites sincere,
Where laughter's heard where nobody goes.

The Promise of Eternal Whimsy

There's a rabbit wearing shoes,
With a trumpet, it calls the tune,
While pigeons dance on rooftops,
Singing songs to the brightened moon.

Floors made of bubblegum dreams,
Dance to the rhythm of giggles,
A whale paints rainbows in streams,
While everyone jumps and wriggles.

Balloons wear mustaches with pride,
Each one claims to be a jet,
In the sun-soaked carnival tide,
Where every day's a fun vignette.

As jellyfish float in tuxedos,
The marshmallows wrestle on stage,
We find joy in every pose,
As laughter spins from page to page.

Dreams that Dazzle

A shoe that walks by itself,
Stealing socks from the nightstand,\nChasing dreams in the moonlight,
With giggles written in the sand.

Flying pigs strut with charm,
With capes made from peppermint sticks,
Too busy dishing out warmth,
While they plan all their silly tricks.

Candy canes guard the front gate,
While a gingerbread man runs free,
Oh, the world's a giant plate,
Filled with laughter and mystery.

On clouds where unicorns play,
The popcorn rains down like stars,
In the realm where dreams say yay,
Life's a waltz without any bars.

Threads of Enigma

A turtle dons a top hat's flair,
While juggling apples, he takes a bow,
With party hats upon the air,
Every moment makes you go wow!

Whiskers twitch with a cheeky grin,
As kittens compose a fine ballet,
In the theater where laughs begin,
With nibbles and giggles on display.

Noses painted with polka dots,
Llamas tweeting all the latest news,
In this world, no one forgets,
To sip on rainbows infused with snooze.

As peppermint clouds squish and sway,
All the comets dance in pairs,
With moonlit silliness at play,
Life's a riddle that love declares.

The Charm of Solitude

In quiet corners where giggles play,
The dust bunnies dance, leading me astray.
A sock on the floor with a wink and a grin,
Whispers sweet secrets of the mess within.

Tea time with echoes and laughter of yore,
The cat judges me from its high kitchen floor.
Books stack like dominoes in a charming heap,
In the cozy chaos, my fancies leap.

The Alluring Whisper of Fate

A fortune cookie cracked, oh what a find,
'You will trip on your shoes, but don't lose your mind.'
I chuckle and nod, while the universe stares,
It loves every tumble, it's quite the affair.

With swirling dreams and a hint of delight,
Serendipity giggles, lighting up the night.
A dance with my friends, oh, what a grand sight,
We joke 'bout the fumbles that make us feel right.

Riddles in the Night

The moon winks down with a mischievous gleam,
As shadows of limericks float in a dream.
A squirrel with a hat, a raccoon that can rhyme,
Tell tales of wonder, all wrapped up in time.

Stars giggle softly, they've secrets to share,
While the night air tickles with a playful dare.
'Find me a riddle,' the darkness might tease,
And laughter erupts like a fresh, buzzing breeze.

Infatuation with the Arcane

In dusty old tomes where the magic is sly,
A dragon named Lou, with a twinkle in eye.
He brews up a potion, with sprinkles and glee,
While I stand nearby, plotting what might be.

A wand that's a candy, spells made of fun,
The charms backfire, oh where has it run?
With giggles and sparks, my mishaps unfold,
Infatuation glimmers, turning life to gold.

The Spark of the Unknown

In a town where cats wear hats,
And dogs play chess on welcome mats.
A squirrel juggles acorns with grace,
While pigeons gossip all over the place.

The trees dance lightly in the breeze,
Whispering secrets that tease and please.
A man in stripes sells dreams on toast,
While laughing at the ghost of a boast.

Each door flings open with a squeak,
As rubber ducks in rows start to speak.
The sun tickles clouds in playful jest,
In this quirky land, you're truly blessed.

So join the fun, don't stay aloof,
Meet the giraffe who can sing a goof.
With laughter echoing all around,
In the spark of the unknown, joy is found.

Enigmatic Horizons

A walrus with a monocle stares,
At dancing shoes on polar bears.
The sun wears shades, strutting in style,
While ice cream trucks come every mile.

Kites sail on laughter, wild and free,
Tugging at hearts with whimsical glee.
Tickling the clouds with jokes galore,
Who knew the sky could be such a chore?

Balloons take flight in a silly race,
Chasing the moon, oh, what a chase!
Among the mysteries of day and night,
The horizon winks, a delightful sight.

So embrace the joy that hangs in the air,
Find riddles wrapped in a curious dare.
With every oddity, life's a surprise,
In these enigmatic horizons, joy lies.

The Lure of the Heart's Desire

A dancing cupcake caught my eye,
With sprinkles that made the clouds sigh.
Chocolate rivers on a candy shore,
Tales of sweetness forevermore.

A llama with glasses reads the news,
While penguins strut in colorful shoes.
Each step is a pirouette of delight,
In this parade of whimsical sight.

A cat in pajamas takes the lead,
With laughter and antics, as all succeed.
Marshmallow clouds float overheard,
In a world where nonsense is the word.

So follow the path where giggles abide,
Where silly dreams dance and slide.
In this place of laughter and cheer,
The lure of desire is always near.

Rapture in the Realm of Dreams

In slumber's embrace, I ride a snail,
While dancing mice weave a fairy tale.
A cat in a hat offers me a sip,
Of fizzy lemonade from a candy drip.

With stars on their backs, the kittens frolic,
Their giggles echo, pure and iconic.
A marshmallow cloud serves as my bed,
While jellybean birds sing songs in my head.

Gleam of the Mysterious

A shadowy figure with polka-dot shoes,
Offers me cookies, with no time to snooze.
I twirl and I whirl, can't help but grin,
As the sugar rush brings a cheeky spin.

The clock strikes twelve, and what do I see?
A band of owls playing jazz with glee.
They hoot out a rhythm that tickles my toes,
While rocking in trees, where the wild wind blows.

Heartstrings Entwined

With laughter like bubbles, we dance through the air,
A tangle of giggles, with no space to spare.
The mimes play charades of love and despair,
While juggling cupcakes without a care.

In this whimsical world, where odd things reside,
A pig with a parasol takes me for a ride.
We cruise through the puddles of shimmering light,
Chasing rainbow fish that flash with delight.

The Siren's Call

On a beach of marshmallows, I hear a sweet tune,
A mermaid in sunglasses dances by the moon.
With seashells for earrings and laughter that glows,
She pulls me to depths where the jellyfish flows.

She sings of a world where the silly prevails,
And all of our troubles are wrapped up in veils.
With each playful note, my worries all flee,
In this frothy embrace, I'm happy and free.

Magic in the Mundane

In a world where laundry spins,
The socks conspire, hiding sins.
The toaster pops with glee and cheer,
I dance with crumbs, my only fear.

The cat performs a daring leap,
Then tumbles down, it makes me weep.
Spilled coffee on the table's face,
A playful reminder of my race.

The dust bunnies plot their schemes,
While I, a hero, chase my dreams.
The couch cushions hide treasures rare,
A remote control? Oh, what a scare!

In dishes stacked, I find my muse,
Washing them's like singing blues.
A magic spell in every bite,
Life's little joys, my heart's delight.

Enigma's Embrace

The fridge hums with secrets near,
A yogurt cup, what's hiding here?
I open wide, a wafting smell,
This mystery, I know too well.

The garden gnomes all wink and nod,
At squirrels who dance like little gods.
Pans clang like cymbals in a band,
Culinary chaos, quite unplanned.

A post-it note, it tells a tale,
Of laundry lost, and coffee stale.
Each odd reminder brings a laugh,
Like socks that journey on their path.

In this maze of cluttered cheer,
A sock puppet says, 'Come near!'
Life's riddles tucked in mundane life,
Bring laughter through all daily strife.

The Lure of Twilight Shadows

When evening falls, the shadows play,
I chase the cat, who swears she's prey.
A candle flickers, whispers low,
As shadows waltz, they steal the show.

The nighttime snacks are quite the treat,
A dance of chips beneath my feet.
Each crunch a giggle, every bite,
In midnight feasts, my heart takes flight.

Caught in webs of shiny dreams,
The ghost of snacks, or so it seems.
A pair of socks could take the stage,
In this bizarre, spontaneous age.

As laughter echoes through the room,
I twirl a towel, a waving plume.
Every silly moment I can find,
Makes twilight dance, oh so kind.

Bewitched by the Ordinary

A pair of shoes that squeak and slide,
Join me on this zany ride.
The broomstick waits with bated breath,
To foil my plans, a sneaky theft.

The microwave hums like a sage,
Pops corn with fervor, like a stage.
A outfit switch, from drab to fab,
In every mess, I find my fab.

Chasing dust motes in a beam,
They laugh at me, as if a dream.
With every sweep, I stir the air,
And conjure up a strange affair.

The world spins 'round in silly glee,
Each moment holds a mystery.
The magic lies in what we see,
In ordinary, wild revelry.

Secrets Beneath the Surface

Underneath a bubbly foam,
Whispers play like a funny gnome.
Treasure chests with silly pranks,
Dive deeper, find the jester's banks.

Bubbles burst with giggly tunes,
Secrets swirl like dancing loons.
A hidden world of playful jest,
Where laughter's gold is truly blessed.

Fishes wear their sassy hats,
Snapping jokes at dozing spats.
Currents swirl with chuckles bright,
In this realm of pure delight.

So, dive right in, take a chance,
Join the fish in their silly dance.
For beneath the calm and blue,
Lies a joy just waiting for you.

The Glittering Veil

Behind the curtain, sparkles gleam,
A world where nothing's as it seems.
With winks and nods, we share a grin,
As secrets hide with a playful spin.

Feathers float on laughter's breeze,
In this haven, hearts find ease.
Glitter bombs and fab confetti,
Dancing chaos, oh so petty!

Masks adorned with silly flair,
Each step brings giggles, light as air.
Unravel tales that twist and twine,
In this mirthful realm, all is fine.

So pull the strings and let them fly,
Embrace the sparkle, oh my, oh my!
Listen closely for the chime,
In laughter's glow, we've got the time.

Captive of the Elusive

In shadows cast, a figure peeks,
With a grin that softly speaks.
Elusive giggles drifting by,
Tickle fights beneath the sky.

Hurdles jump in witty jest,
Each pursuit—a silly quest.
Catch a glimpse, then off it flies,
Mysteries wrapped in playful sighs.

Chasing giggles through the night,
Twists and turns, what a sight!
For every clue's a hearty laugh,
In this curious, cheeky path.

With every step, the chase ignites,
In this game of silly sights.
A flurry of joy—a friendly tease,
Captive to fun, we aim to please.

The Dance of Intrigue

Under the moon, shadows prance,
Fools and jesters share a glance.
With every twirl, a scheme unfolds,
In this dance where laughter holds.

Footsteps light like popping corn,
In a world where gags are born.
Each spin reveals a secret step,
Mischief grows with every prep.

A waltz of whimsy leads the way,
As jests and giggles weave and sway.
Catch the rhythm, join the fun,
For in this chaos, we have won.

With playful whispers, plans are spun,
This dance of life is never done.
We raise our glasses, toast the night,
In this realm where joy takes flight.

A Glimpse of the Impossible

In a world where squirrels wear hats,
And pigeons debate like friendly spats,
I tiptoe lightly on clouds of cheese,
With giggles spilling in the gentle breeze.

A fish with wings, it flew past me,
Saying, "Join my dance, it's quite the spree!"
I laughed so hard, I fell on the ground,
As jellybeans sprouted all around.

The trees wore socks, they swayed in style,
And every step learned to wear a smile,
With kooky tunes floating through the air,
The whimsical world was beyond compare.

So let's embrace the silly and bright,
In this merry chaos, joy takes flight,
For in this strange, peculiar place,
Laughter thrives with every trace.

The Enchantment of Existence

A toaster sang a morning tune,
As a cat in shades played the bassoon,
With buttered toast that danced around,
In this kitchen, joy could be found.

The clock ticked backwards, what a sight,
As elephants twirled in delight,
Each hour a laugh, each minute a cheer,
In this realm, there was nothing to fear.

Cupcakes flew, with sprinkles galore,
A delightful show, oh, what a score,
I twirled with glee, my heart on a spree,
In this land where nonsense roamed free.

So here's to the fun, the quirky, and weird,
Where laughter and magic are never feared,
In every corner, surprises await,
Join the dance, don't hesitate!

Mirage of the Soul

In the desert where teapots sing,
A mirage comes with a zany fling,
Sand dunes giggle in playful jest,
As shadows play hide and seek with the rest.

A dancing cactus winks at the sun,
While mirage mirth invites everyone,
Camels in tutus waltz through the sand,
This silly spectacle is quite unplanned.

Bubbles of laughter fill the air,
With gummy bears pretending to care,
As sunflowers wear party hats tight,
A festival of joy, pure delight.

So let's wander through this amusing dream,
Where every laugh reigns supreme,
In a landscape that's bound to enthrall,
With quirky wonders that beckon us all.

Curiosity of the Heart

A curious heart, with eyes so wide,
Chased after butterflies that seemed to glide,
Through fields of giggles, bright and bold,
With stories of nonsense just waiting to be told.

Lollipops danced and candy canes swirled,
In a carnival realm, oh, what a world!
With every step, tickles abound,
In the marvelous mayhem, joy is found.

A rabbit wearing sneakers hops near,
As ticklish surprises ignite our cheer,
With balloons that float singing a tune,
Let's frolic together beneath the moon!

For in this wacky, whimsical space,
Curiosity blooms with every trace,
So follow your heart, let it embark,
On this journey of laughter, a joyful spark.

Glimmering Allure of the Night

Stars giggle up high, they wink and sway,
Moonlights tickle the trees in a playful ballet.
Shadows dance with delight, in a moonlit spree,
Whispers of the night are laughing, carefree.

Fireflies flash their neon smiles, oh what a sight,
Night owls cracking jokes, taking flight.
Bats in tuxedos, zooming with flair,
Even the crickets are trying their pair.

Laughter's the tune that the crickets hum,
As starlight paints whoopee cushions of fun.
What a riot, this glorious scene,
Where silliness thrives, in glow and sheen.

Mystique in Every Breath

In shadows where the oddest things lurk,
A frog in a top hat goes out for a quirk.
Balloons float about, losing their way,
While giggles escape, as they start to sway.

Mysterious whispers glide past your ear,
A squirrel in a bowtie, oh my, what's here?
Each breeze carries tales, with a wink and a grin,
Inviting us in where the ruckus begins.

Every step feels like a code to decode,
As footsteps echo in festive abode.
Laughter's the secret, it shines and it brews,
In the realm of the odd, joy's what you choose.

Threads of Intrigue

Webs of whimsy are spun in the air,
A spider who knits keeps us unaware.
Jellybeans tumble, rolling in glee,
Flavored like nonsense, just wait and see!

Mystifying puppets pull strings with finesse,
A jester jumps high, in a bright polka dress.
Each twist and each turn is a riddle to crack,
Baffling the wise, while the silly sneak back.

With hats full of giggles, we're bound to collide,
In a carnival world where fun takes a ride.
Follow the antics, chase butterflies sweet,
As laughter's the thread that makes us complete.

Essence of the Ethereal

Clouds wearing sombreros dance 'round in the sky,
A cat with a lollipop woos birds passing by.
When giggles become bubbles, they float ever near,
It's magic, it's mayhem, it's laughter we hear.

Echoes of chuckles bounce off of the trees,
As fluttering giggles ride on the breeze.
Unicorns snicker as they gallop through mist,
Creating a legend, too grand to resist.

With whimsy as our compass, we float on our way,
Chasing the sparkle that's here to stay.
In a realm where the outlandish rules every laugh,
We find joy in the echoes, a glorious path.

Drawn to the Unseen

In shadows where the secrets play,
A giggle whispers, come what may.
The laughter tickles, gives a nudge,
To peek behind the playful fudge.

A ghost might dance in silly shoes,
While wise owls share their chance to snooze.
The dark holds jokes, both bright and bold,
Like stories from the wise of old.

A twinkling star takes center stage,
With cosmic jokes of every age.
We laugh at quirks of fate's fine art,
For mischief lingers in the heart.

So come, let's wander where we roam,
In realms where laughter feels like home.
The unseen world is full of cheer,
With quirky friends who draw us near.

The Allure of the Night Sky

Look up! The stars are playing tricks,
With moonlit jokes and stardust flicks.
A comet zooms by just to tease,
It tugs at dreams with cosmic breeze.

The Milky Way spills tales untold,
Of space oddities both brave and bold.
A meteor shower might just be
Cats tossing yarn from eternity.

In every twinkle, giggles hide,
The universe holds laughter wide.
So let's play tag with shooting stars,
We'll trade our wishes, count our scars.

Amongst the planets, joy is found,
With jokes that swirl and dance around.
So gaze above, see what they share,
In the night sky, laughter is rare.

Mystical Embrace

In a forest deep where fairies hum,
A wild rabbit plays on a drum.
With trees that giggle as they sway,
And bushes plotting games to play.

The breeze tells secrets, whispers bright,
Of silly sprites that dance at night.
They trip and tumble in delight,
Making friends with owls in flight.

A broomstick's joke, it flies askew,
While flowers giggle at the dew.
Each rustle hides a funny tale,
With winks exchanged like ships set sail.

Embrace the charms of leafy lanes,
Let laughter wash away your pains.
In nature's warmth, we find our place,
In mystical blunders, time we chase.

The Lure of Forgotten Paths

Worn cobblestones beneath our feet,
Lead us back to laughter sweet.
Where squirrels chatter without shame,
And every shadow seems to claim.

An old signpost with a painted grin,
Points to places where mischief's been.
The road may twist, but we won't mind,
For silly surprises we will find.

A fountain spills with playful jest,
Where wishes pop like bubbles, blessed.
With echoes of laughter in the air,
Each step we take, a playful dare.

So join the wander, skip along,
In every corner, we belong.
For every path is filled with cheer,
In forgotten ways, we find our year.

Dance of the Unearthly

In a forest where the shadows play,
A squirrel wore a hat, bright and gay.
He danced with twirls, all limbs a-flail,
While rabbits giggled, telling a tale.

The moon gave glitter, the stars took flight,
As owls hooted jokes that felt just right.
With each awkward move, the trees did sway,
Nature joined in, what a wacky display!

A fox in a tutu found his groove,
While mushrooms bounced to the quirky move.
In this wild ball, no rule applied,
Just laughter echoing far and wide.

So come join the fun, don't be shy,
In the dance of the unearthly, oh my!
With every misstep, spirits will rise,
In a whimsical world where joy never dies.

Siren's Call of Wonder

In the sea where fish dress bold,
A crab recited jokes, being quite bold.
'Knock knock,' he said with a wink and grin,
The seaweed chuckled, let the fun begin!

Mermaids played cards with a sea horse man,
While a dolphin juggled, oh what a plan!
Each splash of foam brought giggles anew,
As octopuses danced in a briny blue.

A starfish tripped, it couldn't recover,
While jellyfish spun like no other.
'Why did the turtle cross the sea?'
To have a laugh, just you and me!

So heed the call, don't swim away,
In the siren's laughter, join the play.
With bubbles of cheer, let your heart soar,
In this whimsical realm, you'll find much more.

Lattice of Enchantment

In a garden filled with colors bright,
Ladybugs wore bows, a curious sight.
With flowers gossiping, petals aflame,
Each whisper of joy had a silly name.

A gnome on stilts tried to reach the sky,
While butterflies laughed, oh me, oh my!
They flitted about, in a playful craze,
As bees hummed tunes in a wacky phase.

In this lattice where silliness bloomed,
A cat in sunglasses basked, well-groomed.
'Why sit and pout?' asked a wise old tree,
When laughter's the remedy, come share with me!

So twirl in this wonder, let your heart sing,
For life's too short not to wear a spring ring.
In this wacky garden, let giggles prevail,
In the layers of laughter, we'll joyfully sail.

Essence of the Enchanted

In a realm where the bumblebees dream,
A hedgehog wore glasses, what a theme!
He read from a book, upside down, of course,
While snails played chess, a slow-moving force.

With pixies fluttering, hair like spun gold,
They swapped secret potions for stories bold.
And frogs sang ballads, so off-key,
As fireflies blinked in quirky spree.

A wise old owl wore a powdered wig,
While dancing on branches, did a little jig.
'What's the key to laughter?' a fox quipped sly,
'To never take life too seriously, oh my!'

So gather your friends in this whimsical land,
In the essence of folly, hand in hand.
With giggles and grins, let adventure unfold,
In this enchanted world, be joyful and bold!

Enchanted Echoes of the Heart

In a land where giggles reign,
A pickle danced on a silver plane.
Moonlight chuckled, stars did wink,
Hearts flew high with every clink.

With frogs in tutus, prancing near,
And toads reciting rhymes sincere.
Laughter rippled through the air,
In this world, all joys to share.

A snail with glasses read a book,
While wise old owls just laughed and shook.
Tickled toes on marshmallow ground,
In silly hats, the fun was found.

So let us dance on rainbows bright,
Chasing giggles through the night.
In this realm where silly's king,
Hearts take flight on laughter's wing.

Pull of the Unfathomable

A cat in a hat, so very spry,
Jumps high for cookies that float in the sky.
With jellybeans raining down from the moon,
He sings to the stars a ridiculous tune.

The fish in the pond wear glasses of gold,
While ducks in tuxedos spin tales of old.
Under the surface, a party unfolds,
With secrets and laughter, the merriment molds.

Worms in a conga line wiggle with glee,
As ants throw confetti way up in the tree.
In this crazy, curious scene,
Who knew the garden could be so keen?

Chasing shadows that giggle and dart,
It's a world where whimsy springs from the heart.
So come take a trip through this peculiar place,
And dance with the odd in a wild, funny race!

Delight in the Unexpected

A pickle played poker, what a surprise,
With a bunny dealer and firefly eyes.
Chips made of cheese stacked high to the brim,
In the game of the century, who'll take the whim?

A fox in a skirt juggled lemons with flair,
While giggling gophers gave cheers from the chair.
The night air crackled with playful delight,
As laughter bounced high like balloons in flight.

A cupcake burst forth with sprinkles galore,
While the moon did a shimmy behind a sly door.
What joy, what fun, what a sight to behold,
When sweetness and laughter came dancing bold.

So let's frolic in fields where the quirky collide,
With cheer and with joy magnified wide.
For in the odd corners of life, we discover,
The magic awaits; it's just waiting to hover!

Secrets on the Breeze

The whispers of wind tell stories untold,
Of squirrels sipping cocoa, so daring and bold.
They flip through pages of laughter and cheer,
In a world where even shadows can sneer.

A breeze tickles flowers, making them giggle,
While ants in top hats perform a jiggle.
Bubbles afloat with secrets so sweet,
Fluttering 'round on whimsical feet.

Clouds wear pajamas, drifting off slow,
While raindrops decide to put on a show.
The sun beams a smile, and the moon gives a nod,
In this place of wonder, nothing feels odd.

So catch all the stories that rustle and play,
In the dance of the leaves as they sway and sway.
For magic is found in every small thing,
In the laughter of life, let your spirit take wing!

Caught in the Spell of Now

In the swirl of bright confetti,
I tripped on my shoelace, oh so petty.
Laughter burst like soda pop,
As I danced till I could flop.

Ice cream cones spun a sticky tale,
A banana split that tipped the scale.
Juggling nuts with a wobbly grin,
Who knew chaos could feel like a win?

Tickles of sunshine play on the ground,
Jumping in puddles with grace I found.
Wiggling toes in soggy shoes,
Every moment a headline news.

In a world full of quirky sights,
My hat flew off in a gusty fight.
Chasing after it with all my might,
What a scene, oh what a sight!

Irresistible Journey

On a train made of gummy bears,
We chugged along without any cares.
Each seat a marshmallow, oh so sweet,
With every bump, we bounced on our feet.

A squirrel in a tux made quite the toast,
As penguins danced, we laughed the most.
Chocolate rivers flowed with delight,
In a world where wrong feels so right.

Sipping fizzy tea from nutty cups,
Fluffy clouds took us high up and up.
A rollercoaster made of dreams,
With silly giggles and silly screams.

With every giggle, we hugged the air,
This trip is strange, but we don't care.
Blissfully lost in our sweet refrain,
As we reroute back on the candy train!

The Lure of Infinite Possibilities

What if frogs wore tiny hats?
Or kittens knew how to chat?
In a world where wishes bloom,
Every corner brings more room.

A pie flew by and winked at me,
I caught it quick, oh what glee!
Balloons that giggle, how they tease,
With every glance, they dance with ease.

Silly creatures prance and sway,
In the sunshine's warm display.
What if clouds could cook and bake?
A fluffy breakfast for the taking!

With dreams like candy in the sky,
We chased them down, oh my oh my!
Each step a chance for hearty chuckles,
In a place where laughter buckles!

Where Secrets Lie

In a closet full of shoes too blue,
I found a hat that knew the view.
Whispers floated like a breeze,
Tales of nonsense brought us to our knees.

Under the stairs where shadows peek,
A garden gnome began to speak.
With every rhyme, we spun a tale,
Where giggles sprouted without fail.

Cupcakes held a mystery sweet,
With every bite, we'd dance on our feet.
Behind each corner, we'd always find,
Secrets that tickled the curious mind.

In the world of oddities and glee,
Every turn, a new jubilee.
Between the cracks and shadows sly,
Laughter's where the secrets lie!

Whirlwind of Dreams

In a spin of bright colors,
Laughter dances in the air,
Wondrous wishes just float by,
Chasing joy without a care.

A sprinkle of absurdity,
Tickles the mind, oh so free,
Jumping puddles of pure nonsense,
Life's a jolly jubilee.

Mice in hats and laughing turtles,
Whirling past with silly grins,
Each twist adds a little sparkle,
Giggles rise, the fun begins.

We spin in circles of delight,
Twirling in a dizzy haze,
In this carnival of laughter,
Every moment, an outrageous maze.

Entwined in Fortune's Grasp

With a wink and a cheeky smile,
Fortune waltzes, what a scene,
Raining confetti made of giggles,
Luck's a jester, so obscene.

Fortunes jump like frogs at play,
Hopping, leaping to surprise,
Each misstep is just a game,
Life's crazy, no need for ties.

Come dine with whimsy and charm,
The table's set with playful snacks,
A platter of wild mishaps,
Laughter woven in the cracks.

With each sip of joy's fine nectar,
We toast to the whims we possess,
A dance with fortune's strange embrace,
In this chaos, we find success.

The Temptation of the Unknown

Peeking through the secret door,
Curiosity calls my name,
What lies beyond this warped mirror?
Is it candy or is it lame?

Strings of fate pull gently on me,
Tugging at my silly heart,
The unknown's a mischievous trick,
Where adventure plays its part.

Monkeys swing and shout hello,
As I skip on clouds of fluff,
Every corner hides a giggle,
Is this place just a bit too tough?

Wrapped in whispers of delight,
Mysteries prance on little feet,
With a chuckle and a cheer,
Embrace the unknown, feel the beat.

The Serene Pull of Mystery

In shadows where the giggles hide,
The silly secrets start to bloom,
Each chuckle echoes in the dark,
In laughter's cozy, warm room.

Luna sings a song of secrets,
Her voice is sweet, like candy treats,
We swirl like leaves in autumn's sway,
Mysteries dance on playful beats.

The enigma giggles in disguise,
A riddle wrapped in sprightly cheer,
What will unfold in this soft haze?
The answer's never quite so clear.

With a wink, we chase the whispers,
Stumbling through a twilight glow,
In each mystery lies a jest,
Where laughter's river freely flows.

The Dance of Shadows and Light

Beneath the moon, shadows play,
With giggles and whispers, they sway.
Light flickers like a mischievous sprite,
Chasing the dark in a hilarious fight.

The trees are all laughing, they shimmy and shake,
As stars sprinkle wishes, and wishes forsake.
A dance that's so silly, you can't help but grin,
With shadows and light, let the playground begin!

A bug with a bow tie slips in a puddle,
While a glowworm sings, making everyone huddle.
The breeze joins the fun and gives a soft shove,
In this waltz of the night, we find a new love.

As dawn peeks in, the laughter won't fade,
The dance carries on, in the light's masquerade.
With giggles and shadows, the world spins around,
For in every chuckle, the magic is found.

Magic Woven in Silence

In silence they gather, the quirkiest crew,
Knitting enchantments from laughter and dew.
With needles of starlight and thread made of dreams,
They stitch up the night with whimsical themes.

A cat with a monocle takes a fine seat,
As owls in bowties join in for a treat.
Whispers of mischief float on the breeze,
As everyone snickers while hiding with ease.

The silence it swells with a tickle of glee,
As one bumps a table, spills tea with a spree.
The potions all bubble, then splash with a pop,
In a chorus of giggles, the fun will not stop.

With every soft rustle, a secret revealed,
The magic they weave, all laughter concealed.
In this light-hearted moment, they flourish and twine,
For the laughter of night is truly divine.

The Heart's Hidden Compass

There's a compass that dances in beats of the heart,
Leading us where all the giggles impart.
We follow the arrows with whims and delight,
To find joy in the corners, where shadows ignite.

With maps made of sparkles and trails of sweet tunes,
We venture forth wildly, like puppies in dunes.
Each giggle a beacon, a sign from above,
Our compass spins wildly, directing our love.

The sun's winks at us as we sway side to side,
In this place of wonder, there's nothing to hide.
The compass stops spinning, we're lost in the thrill,
In the heart's merry dance, we've found our goodwill.

And maybe the secret, we've found on this way,
Is that laughter's the compass that guides our play.
So follow those giggles, let joy be the map,
For in this adventure, we're all in the lap.

Drawn to the Twilight Realm

In twilight's embrace, the silliness blooms,
With fairies in hats and some goofy raccoons.
The sky winks at me, swirling hues of delight,
Where laughter's a lantern, illuminating the night.

The rabbits wear shoes and boast quite the style,
As they hop to the beat and dance all the while.
Each step is a joke, with a punchline that gleams,
In this realm of the twilight, where laughter redeems.

The stars shine like disco balls up in the sky,
While crickets play maracas, all flippant and spry.
As night settles in, the antics unfold,
In this place of mischief, the stories are told.

So join in the frolic, let worries take flight,
For the twilight holds secrets that sparkle in light.
With giggles and glee, let's dance till it's dawn,
In the realm of the funny, forever we're drawn.

The Spell of Timeless Moments

In a world where clocks do play,
Time dances on a sunny day.
Each tick and tock is oh so sly,
As hours waltz with butterflies.

We jump through hoops and spin around,
In this circus where joy is found.
Pretzels twist and laughter soars,
We lose our shoes and search for doors.

With ice cream smiles and silly grins,
We race the breeze and seek our wins.
In every wink, a playful tease,
As giggles float upon the breeze.

So grab a friend and let's not stop,
We'll ride the wave till we drop.
In this magic, fun entwines,
In timeless moments, joy defines.

In the Garden of Wonders

In a garden where giggles grow,
Wondrous things begin to show.
Daisies wear their sunshine hats,
While squirrels play leapfrog with the cats.

Ladybugs in polka dots,
Dance on stems and tie up knots.
A fountain sings a silly tune,
As frogs croon to the light of the moon.

Bubbles float like whispered dreams,
Tickling the air with sparkly beams.
Each flower holds a secret laugh,
As bumblebees take bubble baths.

So wander here, forget your cares,
In this place with sunny flares.
A world where mischief softly lingers,
Join the fun, and twirl your fingers.

Connections in the Ether

In the ether where thoughts collide,
Laughter takes a joyful ride.
Messages wrapped like candy bars,
Whisk us off to dance with stars.

Jokes taken lightly, like a breeze,
Float around with silly ease.
With each nudge and gentle poke,
The universe begins to joke.

Fingers point and giggles soar,
As whispers echo, never bore.
Ideas bounce like rubber balls,
Making sense behind the walls.

So herein lies our merry quest,
To find connection—don't you jest!
The ether buzzes with delight,
As we share laughs beneath the night.

Embraced by Ethereal Radiance

In a glow where chuckles beam,
Light wraps us up in a sweet dream.
Sparkles dance on open air,
As joy twirls everywhere.

With every echo of our cheer,
The stars align, they simply peer.
As we frolic, and thoughts ignite,
Brimming laughter paints the night.

Floating high on whimsy's wings,
Surreal moments, oh what it brings!
With puns and jests that wiggle free,
We create our own jubilee.

So take a leap beyond the norm,
In this glow, let happiness swarm.
Embraced by light, we're ever bold,
In radiant laughs, life unfolds.

Echoes of Hidden Magic

In a world where socks do roam,
They dance alone, far from home.
With a wink, they start to sway,
Trying hard to seize the day.

Mismatched shoes with quirky flair,
Whisper secrets in the air.
Fluffy kittens hold a truce,
Hatching schemes with every moose.

Lawn gnomes giggle in the night,
It's their time to start a fight.
Squirrels plotting mischief bold,
Stealing treasures, joyful, and gold.

When the moon spills silver light,
Worms wear hats, oh what a sight!
Life is silly, laughter bright,
In this realm of pure delight.

A Dance with the Unfathomable

A cat in a hat takes a spin,
Twirling about with a cheeky grin.
The dog joins in, a clumsy leap,
As the world around begins to creep.

Cupcakes sing with frosting bright,
While jellybeans engage in a fight.
The sun winks from high above,
A silly waltz, full of love.

Clouds wear shoes, so round and fluffy,
In this play, nothing's too stuffy.
Bouncing rainbows, what a show!
You never know where giggles flow.

Balloons float with pompous flair,
Sipping tea from fancy air.
Laughter echoes, round the bend,
In this dance, there's no end.

The Soft Touch of Illusion

A penguin prances on a screen,
Wearing shades, looking quite keen.
Seagulls chuckle with delight,
As the flippered chap takes flight.

Spaghetti slurps with glee,
Hitching rides on a bumblebee.
A noodle party in the sun,
With giggles echoing, oh what fun!

Brushes paint without a thought,
Making hats from what they sought.
Pasta shapes and noodle ties,
Dancing under noodle skies.

Oranges swing in perfect arcs,
Dropping jokes with little sparks.
Life's a circus, can't you see?
With winks and laughs from you and me.

Touched by the Otherworldly

A ghost with style rocks the floor,
Gliding past, then back for more.
Glamorous in a sheet so white,
Stealing snacks in the dead of night.

Witches swirl on broomstick rides,
Chasing frogs, they laugh and glide.
A potion brewed, but tastes so odd,
It bubbles up and gives a nod.

Mice in boots, a joyful crew,
On tiny bikes, they paddle through.
Join the fun, don't be shy,
In this realm where laughter flies.

Fairies giggle, sprinkle dust,
Turning acorns into rust.
Winks exchanged, it's all in play,
In this world of whimsical sway.

Veils of Hypnotic Beauty

In a dazzling dress, she spins around,
Her laughter echoes, a joyful sound.
The crowd is lost, caught in her glee,
Like moths to a flame, they can't help but see.

With a wink and a grin, she pulls them near,
Twirling and whirling, shedding all fear.
A spell of silliness weaves through the air,
As she juggles bananas without a care.

Each flip of her hair, a colorful flight,
The world feels lighter in her playful sight.
Bubblegum popping, she dances with ease,
Even the statues begin to tease.

What magic is this that wraps us so tight?
A carnival ride on a whimsical night.
In veils of delight, she reigns supreme,
Chasing us down in a giggling dream.

Whispers in the Wind

A breeze carries laughter on the sly,
As clouds play hide and seek in the sky.
A squirrel in shades, prances with flair,
While ducks in bowties waddle with care.

"Hey, what's the rush?" the daisies declare,
With petals that chatter, they just don't care.
The grass tickles toes with a mischievous jig,
As butterflies dance, wearing hats quite big.

Whispers of giggles swirl all around,
Each rustle of leaves, a secret profound.
Laughter escapes from the bark of a tree,
Where even the owls wink playfully.

What fun to be caught in this blustery game,
Each gust carries hints that tease just the same.
In this playful romp, the world feels so light,
As whispers in the wind take off in delight.

Threads of Enchantment

A needle of humor weaves tales so grand,
With threads of laughter spun by a hand.
Each stitch a story, bright colors combined,
A tapestry of giggles skillfully aligned.

In a patchwork of whimsy, patterns unfold,
With polka dots dancing, so bold and so gold.
The seamstress twirls, her fabric a sea,
As frogs in bowler hats join in with glee.

Quilting the clouds with a glittering thread,
She stitches the sunshine, the daisies ahead.
With crayons in hand, she colors the night,
In threads of enchantment, everything's right.

A playful parade, each row hand-stitched,
Where rabbits in tuxedos feel blissfully bewitched.
As laughter spills forth from her magical loom,
In a bright tapestry, we all feel the bloom.

Fascination in Dappled Light

Underneath the trees where the shadows play,
A squirrel in sunglasses steals the day.
Bubbles float high, glitter in the sun,
Where even the ants stop to join in the fun.

Dappled light dances in rays of delight,
As frogs on a lily pad croak out a rite.
With cheeky chirps, the birds sing along,
Creating a chorus that feels like a song.

Caught in the moment, the whole world glows,
With a sprinkle of magic wherever it goes.
Sunbeams tickle the cheeks of the trees,
As laughter drifts softly upon the breeze.

What whimsy exists in this magical spot?
A kingdom of joy—oh, forget-me-not!
In fascination found in dappled delight,
Life spins like a carousel, merry and bright.

Elysian Reveries at Dawn

In morning's glow, we dance and prance,
With silly hats and shoes askew,
A chocolate breeze, a spongecake chance,
We giggle loud, just me and you.

The sun, a jester, winks with glee,
As toast flies high from buttered plates,
With every sip of syrupy tea,
We conjure joy, no room for waits.

Clouds wearing polka dots just for fun,
They twirl around in a playful chase,
Each moment stitched, a quirky pun,
Laughter echoes in this sunlit space.

So let us prance, we'll steal the day,
In this bright realm where smiles abide,
A whimsical world, come what may,
Where all our giggles will coincide.

Enchanted Whispers

In gardens sweet where whispers bloom,
The flowers gossip in a cheer,
With twirling bees that play and zoom,
And every giggle filled with beer.

A squirrel wears a tiny hat,
While rabbits dance, an awkward sight,
They sing of cheese and chase a bat,
Under the watchful, grinning light.

The moon comes down, a secret guest,
He winks and joins the silly spree,
With twinkling stars in jesting jest,
A sparkling night, wild and free.

Each step a melody in jest,
As shadows tango with the trees,
We find delight in every quest,
In laughter's arms, we take a breeze.

The Allure of Twilight

The sun dips low, a jolly thief,
As evening steals the daylight cheer,
With purple clouds wrapped like a reef,
We race the stars to see what's near.

The crickets croon a goofy tune,
While fireflies flash their neon lights,
We laugh until we're over the moon,
As night descends, with quirky sights.

A shadow prances in the dark,
A dance of giggles, a silly sway,
Where echoes sing and laughter sparks,
United in this twilight play.

So let the night, a mischief-call,
Wrap us tight in its funny fold,
With every stumble, we'll not fall,
In twilight's charm, our tales unfold.

Spellbound in Moonlight

The moon, a clown in silver glow,
Whispers secrets through the night,
As dancing shadows sway in tow,
Competing for the starry light.

With every step, the grass will giggle,
As owls hoot a rhythm divine,
We chase the ghouls, trip and wiggle,
Under the sky, all seems just fine.

A bog's bright frog plays a lute,
The moths join in with wings all spun,
In this odd world, we feel so root,
All fears dissolve, oh what fun!

So come, dear friend, let's take a ride,
In this wild night where dreams take flight,
With laughter's echo as our guide,
We'll revel in this moonlit night.

The Veil of Wonder

In a land where socks just don't match,
The cats play chess, in a crazy patch.
Marshmallows dance on the trees with glee,
While tap-dancing frogs shout, 'Come see me!'

The sun wears shades, looking quite too cool,
While ducks in bow ties waddle by the pool.
A curious snail, wearing a tutu,
Asks, 'Is this the party or just a zoo?'

Noses twitch with laughs and little quakes,
As the jellybeans make lovely cakes.
In this land where everything's bizarre,
Even the stars hum a silly guitar.

So come take a stroll, let the fun unfold,
With whispers of dreams, both new and old.
A giggle, a wink, let tales entwine,
In the veil of wonder, life sparkles divine.

Temptation's Mirage

Through the fields of frosting, we tread light,
With cupcakes smiling, oh what a sight!
A lemonade fountain, sweet and bright,
Invites everyone to frolic in delight.

The lemonade wears a mustache, quite grand,
As unicorns prance, with treats on hand.
But careful, my friend, it's all a ruse,
A mirage of whimsy you might just lose.

Gumdrop clouds drift in the sky so high,
While popcorn kernels wink and sigh.
A dance with confetti, that's pizza coned,
In this mirage, every heart has moaned.

Hold on to your marshmallows, don't let them fly,
For the winds can carry them to the sly.
In this tempting maze of glee and cheer,
We laugh till we cry; it's why we're here.

When Mysteries Sparkle

Under the glow of a glittering moon,
The owls are playing an offbeat tune.
Stars twinkle secrets in the night sky,
As shadows dance and the fireflies sigh.

A riddle's hiding in a potato sack,
Telling tales of a whale dressed in black.
Though puzzling be, it makes us grin,
For laughter is where the magic begins.

The clock strikes seven, but time won't comply,
With a roller-skating hedgehog nearby.
Each twist and turn brings giggles anew,
As we chase our dreams under skies of blue.

So here we are, in a world so spry,
Where mysteries tickle and tickle our eye.
With laughter echoing through sparkling nights,
This whimsical life is full of delights.

Love in the Time of Enchantment

In the garden of quirks where laughs bloom sweet,
The hearts in the air do a jolly repeat.
With teacups that giggle and pie that winks,
While lovebirds debate on how time thinks.

A jester leaps high, juggling bright pears,
While rubber ducks float without any cares.
And oh, what a sight, the clowns sing their tune,
With melodies that make the flowers swoon.

In this maddening dance where nonsense spins,
A candy cane choir sings of wins.
With a twirl and a laugh, the romance unfurls,
As we toast to the magic, let laughter swirl.

So come take my hand, through sweet, silly lands,
We'll skip with the elves, make delight with our plans.
In this time of enchantment where giggles ignite,
Love is the spark that makes everything bright.

Captivated by Stardust

In the closet, dust bunnies dance,
Wearing tiny shoes, they take a chance.
A waltz of whiskers, a jig of fluff,
I join their party, can't get enough!

The moon winks down with a playful grin,
While socks and shoes start to spin and spin.
Cupcakes bounce on the kitchen floor,
They giggle and say, "Come out for more!"

A cat with a hat, in shades of green,
Sips from a mug, oh what a scene!
He tells me tales of the stars up high,
Where jellybeans and rainbows fly!

In this whimsical world, I lose my mind,
With laughter and candy, it's one of a kind.
So if you see bunnies in your shoes,
Join the fun, you can't refuse!

Enigma of the Enchanter

A wizard once lost a sock, oh dear,
Called a meeting of wands, but no one was near.
His spellbook flipped, filled with snickers,
As the cats in capes shared ghostly flickers.

Balloons floated high in a swing set dream,
While gnomes held a contest of who could scream.
The laughter echoed, a raucous delight,
Even the fireplace joined in the fight!

With potions brewed in a teacup bright,
He conjured a dance, hey, what a sight!
The ghost floated past, gave a wink and a nod,
As everyone laughed, even the odd cod.

A tale spins on about socks gone rogue,
While wizards perform with a sprightly vogue.
Join the gathering where mischief won't end,
In a world where nonsense becomes a friend!

Lured by the Luminance

Flickering lights in a crowded space,
Swapping dessert with a funny face.
A cupcake chased by a nimble fork,
In this silly diner where giggles stalk.

The jukebox plays a wobbly tune,
As plates fly high like a cartoon.
A pancake stack dressed like a clown,
With syrup smiles that won't back down!

A waiter in sparkles, a halo of fries,
Serves up humor that takes to the skies.
While the soda pops bubble with glee,
It's a laughing fit, come share with me!

In this realm of flavors misunderstood,
Find the joy in every food.
So make a toast with a lemon zest cheer,
To the silly moments that keep us near!

The Magic that Beckons

A door that creaks with a squeaky tune,
Opens to chaos, a swirling moon.
Marshmallows whisper in soft-spoken sways,
Telling tales of lunatic days.

A frog in a top hat recites a rhyme,
While candy canes dance, it's almost sublime!
With jellybeans playing leapfrog around,
Their laughter resounds, a joyous sound.

The grass has a sparkle, the trees wear a smile,
Cats juggle shadows, oh let's stay awhile!
A bubblegum dragon plays peek-a-boo,
In a world so wild, bright colors ensue!

So follow the laughter where whimsies convene,
In a land where the quirky holds supreme.
Join in the frolic, the nonsense, the glee,
For magic awaits, just wait and see!

Mesmerized by the Enigma

In a land where the oddities play,
Frogs wear hats and sway all day.
With a wink and a giggle, they hop in a line,
Who knew strange could be so divine?

The moon grinned down, a mischievous sight,
As dancing squirrels spun left and right.
With acorns as maracas, they shook with glee,
Who knew nature could throw such a spree?

A rabbit popped out, wearing a shoe,
Said, "Join the fun, there's room for two!"
With a hop and a skip, we joined the parade,
In this world where serious faces had strayed.

Laughter erupted from bushes and trees,
As butterflies played tunes on the breeze.
A picnic of giggles, stacked high with cheer,
Who knew mystery could make us all cheer?

Dance of the Enchanted

Spinning under twinkling stars so bright,
The centaurs danced in the pale moonlight.
With tap shoes made of leaves and pure delight,
They twirled and giggled, oh what a sight!

A fox with a top hat, quite dapper and sly,
Winked at the crowd passing by.
He juggled ripe berries with flair and finesse,
While the owls hooted softly, no need to impress.

When the sun peeked in with its golden rays,
The party just shifted to a bright summer craze.
With lemonade smiles and picnic plans grand,
No dull moments in this enchanted land.

As kites took to the skies, all colors unfurled,
The laughter cascaded, a joy-filled world.
With every hop, skip, and merry refrain,
We danced until twilight etched joy into grain.

A Symphony of Sorcery

A wizard once sneezed, a most magical thing,
Out popped a chorus, all ready to sing!
With melodies tangled, from high notes to thrift,
Every note was a twist, a most curious gift.

The goblins chimed in, with their pots and their pans,
Making music by chance, with their silly plans.
A dragon flew by, just to catch the beat,
Wagging his tail in a dance so sweet.

From bushes emerged a troupe of young mice,
Performing their ballet, oh, wasn't it nice?
They leapt and they spun, in shoes made of cheese,
Who knew such small beings could move with such ease?

With every crescendo, the laughter rang loud,
As merry critters gathered, a jubilant crowd.
A symphony formed, quite odd but divine,
In this concert of whimsy, all revelers align.

Shadows that Envelop

In a patch of shadows, where giggles reside,
The goblins played tricks, quite sly and wide.
With shadows that danced, and laughter that leaped,
The night turned playful as all secrets seeped.

A whispering breeze brought melodies cool,
As fireflies twinkled, illuminating the pool.
With shadows as partners, they twisted and swirled,
A great jest of nature, in laughter unfurled.

Comets of chuckles zipped over the glades,
Casting spells of joy in the light and the shades.
A game of tag started, amongst the tall trees,
Who knew that fun could be caught by the breeze?

In a world wrapped in silliness, bright and bizarre,
Every shadow was joking, each laugh a new star.
With every silly shadow, the moon gave a grin,
As we chased after fun, where the laughter begins.

www.ingramcontent.com/pod-product-compliance
Lightning Source LLC
Chambersburg PA
CBHW060110230426
43661CB00003B/144